Feeling Through A Poet

A Collection of Poetry Inspired by Human Emotions

Madelynn Mccabe

BookLeaf Publishing

India | USA | UK

Made with ❤ on the BookLeaf Publishing Platform
www.bookleafpub.in
www.bookleafpub.com

Dedication

To my love, for always believing in me.

Preface

Dearest Readers,

I invite you on this journey of feeling with me. A tribute to fellow emotional humans and a guide for those who may not feel as much. Whoever you may be, these feelings are for everyone.

Thank you for feeling them with me.

Acknowledgements

Special thanks to family, friends, acquaintances, angels, pets, teachers, professors, enemies, and anyone in between.

I write for everyone.

Thank you for reading,
Madelynn.

1. Fear

Fear creeps in the shadows of my dark room
and looks me in the eyes when it is light again.

Fear grips my hands pulling me back into
its embrace keeping me from moving forwards,
stuck with it until I learn to wiggle free.

Fear is the monster under my bed
and the devil on my shoulder, sometimes my friend
who thinks they know what is best for me.

Fear knows nothing of me.

2. Worry

The spiders in my brain
work tirelessly every night
spinning a web of thoughts
as my head hits the pillow.
I lie there and watch them
through the back of my eyelids
until I can't take it anymore.
They connect thoughts of tomorrow,
the unknown and uncertain future,
to the mistakes of the past and
how they could catch in this web again.
They connect all my memories and
bring up those I had forgotten whether
it was intentionally or accidentally-
the spiders know no reason.
They are just doing their job
creating a beautifully entangled web of **worry**
while I am the one left with it.

3. Doubt

Only when I am certain of something
does a voice whisper through
the cracks of my confidence
telling me lies to discourage me.

Though I know better,
I can't help but listen to the voice
sometimes, because what if
just this once, it is right

Doubt

    Nobody will ever read this poem.

4. Embarrassment

A sudden heat reaches my cheeks
as I question why I would do such a thing.
But you see, the thing was perfectly normal-
embarrassment is not much of a feeling
but a social construct.
You can only feel embarrassed if you think certain
things,
(like what society tells us) are embarrassing.

To hell with **embarrassment**!

It no longer exists if you don't want it to.

5. Shame

I've gone my whole life
wanting to be seen
and all I ever feel
is looked at in the wrong way.
The weight of what I've done,
who I have become
weights heavy on my conscious.
I lie awake at night
dreaming of who I should have been
the things I could have done
and I ask myself,

Why the hell I didn't?

Leaving me **shame**ful for more than just a moment.

6. Guilt

I've done it.

This time
and the last.

But again
I'll pretend
and
tell myself
I didn't.

So I can
lift the **guilt**
off my
shoulders.

7. Irritation

I don't like to be an irritable person
but when the temperature is not just right
or my skin is the slightest bit sticky
and when someone ignores me
or they didn't hear me when
I've repeated myself three times already
and when a bee lands on me
or a fly dances in my face,
gnats attack my forehead
and when a stinkbug crawls through my window
when I get sick suddenly
with heat flashes and cold sweats
and my nose won't stop running
creating a sore from rubbing it
and when the day starts later than I planned
or the plans change suddenly
having to shift my whole day
but when the phone is ringing
and I have no hands left to answer
or when it goes to voicemail the second I can
and when the phone slips from my butter fingers
when I drove hungry an hour away to a restaurant
and then there is an hour wait to be seated
then the food takes another hour

or the food comes out wrong and cold-
there are just so many **irritating** things.

8. Stress

A large portion of my life has been stolen by stress,
weighing me down heavy every moment
I look at my peers
envious
that they don't have to lug around this burden
someone else helps them
while I
drown
in it.

9. Shock

The writer begins a story
and while you may think
you have the pen all figured out
they switch the ink
and all you are left with is
shock.

10. Anger

A slow boil of heat rises
making the hairs on my neck stand
and fists unconsciously clench,
nails biting the skin of my palm.

I begin to shake
feeling as if I might explode
if I do not flip the furniture
of the room I am in ten times over.

Breathing heavy,
trying to calm down
I look around and
only find more reasons

to be

angry.

11. Frustration

a stubbed toe after a long day of walking
or a bad grade after a long right of studying
a dead phone after charging it all night
or a lost phone after a night of partying
a shoe rubbing a half size too small
or flopping off a size too big
a child screaming in a restaurant
or one running right into your knees
a forgotten password after many resets
or *your new password cannot be the same as the old password*
a red light taking too long to switch
or the car in front of you distracted
a professor marking you absent for being late
or assigning multiples things due on the same day
a word you can't pronounce
or a name just at the tip of your tongue

Frustration at the core of it all

12. Disappointment

Disappointment is a reminder
that not every path leads
to what you thought it would
and what we thought we wanted
isn't always what we need.

13. Betrayal

Her friends tell her she looks pretty
but she remembers that one time
a boy had said the same thing
and then she heard him tell his friends
he would never like someone like her.

Someone tells her they love her
but she remembers the last time
someone said that to her
they reached into her chest
grabbed her heart, and shattered it.

He tells her he'll never leave
but she remembers the boy
who said he'd love her forever
but his forever fell short
and he left when things got hard.

The world says she can trust them
but she remembers every time
she put her trust in somebody
they made her regret it and
she'd never make that mistake again.

Betrayal is a lesson we always learn the hard way

15

14. Despair

Despair,

is not so much
feeling

in fact,

it is the lack of it

the pit

of

emptiness

a hole

where feeling once lied.

15. Boredom

My room begins to feel like a cell
four white walls slowly closing in
I check my phone again
though I know it won't ring

I say I like to be alone
until I'm not sure
what to do with myself
bored.

16. Pride

Pride is loud
while being silent
it does not shout or
need acknowledgment
it stands tall
with wide shoulders
and chin to the sky
but in the back row
because it does not
need the attention
It simply exists
and that is
enough

17. Hope

Children believe in princesses and superheroes
the same way grown women believe in love
and men believe they are the heroes.

Our conscious, the part where
the logical thinking happens,
tells them it will never happen.

The other part, however,
tells them there is a small,
glimpse of hope that it could.

Hope is enough to keep trying

18. Excitement

The familiar pit in my stomach
I often mistake for anxiety
I quickly realize
I am not afraid

I am **excited.**

and there are no other words to describe it.

19. Pleasure

A spout of longing
is hushed by lips
meeting in the silence
of bodies speaking
the language of touch,
tongues fighting
for the podium
lingering just enough
to cut the other off
to whisper sweet
pleasures.

20. Joy

Joy fills a room like sunlight
through an open window.

It is shared through toothy grins
and echos through stories told
causing laughter heard from down the hall.

Joy is a gentle reminder
that life is worth it.

21. Serenity

Emotions are like the weather.

They can be calm
then turn into wind
and rain, then a storm
destroying everything
in it's path.

But there's a rainbow after rain
and calm again after a storm,
a peace following chaos

Serenity